Quick Guide VI:
How to Sell Coaching

Number 6 in a series of articles by

Paul C Burr PhD

http://paulcburr.com/

Copyright 2014 Paul C Burr

Acknowledgements

Penelope Walsh, Writer and Editor

Kristen Johnson, Learning and Development Professional

Professor John S Ditch

Other Titles in this Series

Quick Guide - How Top Salespeople Sell

Quick Guide II - How to Spot, Mimic and Become a Top Salesperson

Quick Guide III - How to Bridge the Pillars of Successful Business Relationships

Quick Guide IV – A Scorecard that Accounts for Mindfulness in Business

Quick Guide V - How to Apply Mindfulness to Business Relationships

Books by the Author

For The Love of Lilith & How to Put Love into Practice (and Non-attach Yourself to It)

The Mystique to the Game of Life (and Unrequited Love) - #Mindfulness in Relationships Series No 1

Defrag your Soul

2012: a twist in the tail - a novel

Learn to Love & Be Loved in Return

Contents

PREFACE

INTRODUCTION 1

THE DIFFERENCE BETWEEN COACHING AND CONSULTING/MENTORING 3

WHAT A CLIENT SEEKS: THE OVERARCHING PRINCIPLES 9

HOW TO SETUP YOUR FIRST CALL 10

SELL COACHING IN ONE CALL, VIA *THE INTRODUCTORY SESSION* 11

    1. THE INTERVIEW 11
        First Phase – Quick Run Through 11
        Second Phase – Comments about Each Question 14
    2. PLAYBACK/ REVIEW 23
    3. EXPLAIN WHAT COACHING IS, WHAT IT IS NOT, AND WHAT NEEDS TO HAPPEN TO ASSURE SUCCESS 25
    4. DISCOVER WHAT WILL MAKE COACHING WORTHWHILE 30

CALLING ON AN EXECUTIVE SPONSOR 34

CLOSING NOTES 36

"THANK YOU..." 38

APPENDIX: ABOUT ME, PAUL C BURR I

    THE SKILLS AND PASSIONS IN ME II
    THE AUTHOR IN ME... V

Preface

This booklet, in common with each of my other *Quick Guides to Business,* can be read quickly, in less than an hour.

First and foremost, selling or coaching is about you being the real you, the authentic you, the congruent you – in a space, your client's personal space. The client shares that space with you because they trust your integrity. They let you to lead them beyond the boundaries of that space. They trust your capability to help them in another space that is both uncomfortable and unknown - unknown to them and unknown to you. The most important thing you bring to a meeting is (1) your intention and (2) your integrity. These two facets alone will bring you the success that's right for you and your capabilities.

The sales process within will 'up' what's right for you.

The article bears from my research, consulting, direct selling and coaching within global corporations over a twenty year period. The companies I worked directly for, or in a freelance capacity with, include: IBM, Cisco, Accenture, Xerox, Microsoft, American Express, Standard Chartered, BP and Reckitt Benckiser. During this period I've had the privilege to meet, work with and coach hundreds of top performers worldwide.

Paul C Burr

October 2014

Introduction

I've coached hundreds of people in large and small organisations around the world. I enjoy a higher-than-95% conversion ratio from prospecting to sales with the people who are seeking to be coached personally.

The prime aim of this book is to share with you the what-and-how of...

1. A 'sales' process that can give you a greater than 95% success rate when selling to potential coaching clients.

And answer the question...

2. How is it successful?

Having said the above, you can go straight to the section, *Sell Coaching in One Call, via The Introductory Session*, and test the process out for yourself. It's 'client ready'.

I've met many coaches and consultants who don't like, or feel very competent at, selling. Some of these people held very high offices in large corporations. About 'selling'...

> *"It's not something I would do to a dog."*
> Quote from a Partner in a top-10, world famous, consulting firm.

By a twist of fate, I went from corporate selling into coaching. I started my 'corporate career' in IBM. There I spent sixteen years in sales: starting in sales support, then sales, then sales management, and then developing new career paths to sell consulting services, as opposed to hardware. I now have over thirty years of corporate selling experience. I still consider myself a student in the noble art of 'selling with integrity'.

I call it an 'art' because selling, for me, is two parts emotional to one part intellectual. There may be sound business reasons for a customer to buy from you, yet ultimately they buy from you because what you offer looks right, sounds right and feels right in their mind. Moreover, the customer puts trust in your integrity and capability to deliver what you promise better than anyone else.

Coaching is neither mentoring nor consulting. So I'm going to delineate coaching from what I call these latter two types of 'expert interventions'. Nonetheless, I've found the process I use to be equally valuable when you start the sales dialogue (open and qualify) whether you are selling coaching, mentoring, consulting, therapy, or with a little customisation, any product or service. The same process works whether you are selling business-to-business (B2B) or to an individual client.

The process will take you and the client to a space where they discover if coaching is right for them and you are the right person to coach them. In this space, the client will be completely at ease to say "yes" or "no" to your sales proposition. That is, you make the sale on the first call, or not. Either way, you do it in a manner so that you and the client walk away from the call completely accountable for the outcome.

Like all the other guides in this series, this 'quick-guide' is intended to be read within one hour. If you want a more comprehensive picture of how 'top salespeople' sell and how 'top business relationships' are forged and thrive, I'll point you at other books, as they apply to the text within, that will fill in more of the 'puzzle'.

The Difference between Coaching and Consulting/Mentoring

Coaching is not mentoring. Coaching is not consulting. Coaching is not training. Coaching is not therapy - but it's probably more akin to therapy, and the term 'therapy' is still struggling to find a foothold in corporate cultures where problems are seen as weaknesses.

Coaching is about helping people to make breakthroughs to improve their business or personal performance. The 'coachees' might already be at the top of the 'performance tree', they may be struggling, or (like most people) somewhere in between.

My value proposition is hopefully clear and simple. *"I will help people improve their performance by 30% or more in a matter of weeks, and in some cases, days."*

My definition of coaching, addresses the issues that inhibits clients from making breakthroughs. These issues are almost always emotional issues and not intellectual issues.

Case Study: Me and My Comfort Zones

In my early years in sales, by and large, I got on very well with clients' operations managers. When I met or presented to a client's more senior management, I would do my best to make sure I was structured and grounded my proposals in facts and data. Nonetheless, I often felt nervy and that came across in my body language and in the tonality of my voice. Senior clients would often think to themselves, "Paul does his ground work and thinks things through but he's uncomfortable at this level. If I'm going to take his proposals up the line I'll need to involve someone more senior from his company".

*** End of case study ***

Coaching takes people outside their comfort zone in a safe and secure manner; so that a client is okay if things don't work out the way they want, the first time around. It provides the client with tools to learn equally from successes and setbacks – especially in the domain of relationships. (For a guide to forging excellent business relationships I refer you to *Quick Guide III:*

How to Bridge the Pillars of Successful Business Relationships.)

I have found that business, and life for that matter, is all about relationships, relationships, relationships.

When there is no-one with the power of veto to stop what you're trying to achieve, including yourself, then you cannot fail. You succeed.

Mentoring or consulting, on the other hand implies that you are dealing with an expert; someone who has first-hand experience of new areas in your line of business; experience that you do not have. They might, for example, have studied world-class practice in a new business model in which you wish to engage. They will be capable of identifying the gaps between where you are now and where you wish to be. They will be able to customise a business model that meets your precise needs to fill those gaps. They will transfer skills over to you to fill those gaps, so that at some point in time you no longer feel dependent on their input.

The outcomes for both coaching and mentoring/consulting are the same, improved business performance and improved personal skills. Both get you to do things differently, whether those things are old or new. But the processes of achieving improved business performance are different and often complimentary. Coaching primarily addresses the emotional journey (which is still often overlooked) involved in change, whereas consulting/mentoring primarily addresses its intellectual journey.

The two categories, coaching and consulting/mentoring, require different mindsets: non-expert and expert. The two categories each require a different approach as well, directive and non-directive. I'll explain what I mean by 'non-expert' and 'non-directive' through the following case study and later, when I define what coaching is and is not, to a prospective client.

Case Study – Top 5 Global IT Firm, Managers as Coaches

I coached a European team of managers who were already equipped with/'trained-in' an oft used coaching technique (*GROW: Goal, Reality, Options and Way forward*). BUT, they were not equipped to help their salespeople 'grow' their performance by more than a few percentage points. Going for, say, 30% growth requires a much more profound approach.

It involves taking people though a structured process outside their comfort zone to do some things very differently, often things that in the past, have anxiety associated with them. This level of coaching is not a competence that coaches will pick up in a two/three day training course. It requires that they experience passing though their own anxiety barriers – so that they understand more fully the emotional journey that they'll subsequently be coaching others through – by taking their own 'medicine' first.

Here are testimonies from the sales managers I coached, about what it's like to be coached and subsequently coach people to increase their sales by over 30%. Some refer to specific tools and techniques which they hadn't received in their conventional 'coaching-training'.

- *Coaching requires a completely different mindset. When I use it the process gets an A* for managing poor performers.*
- *Coaching isn't an individual session; it takes place over a period of time to get to a solution. Using '2nd position' (how to stand in another person's shoes) has helped enormously. It's made me face some of my own demons.*
- *I took the material and applied it rigorously to coaching X. The meeting wasn't easy! I faced my demons and got on with it. It's not there yet but the mountain has moved.*
- *I've used the 'Success and Setback Analyses'.* (Two tools that, respectively, 'paint' both sides of the boundary of, or limits to, the success we create for ourselves.) *I've overcome my shyness... I feel I've moved out of my comfort zone.*
- *I am more rigorous in the 'Analytical and Process Quadrants'* (a 'thinking preferences' analytical tool) *and it's paid off.*
- *I took away the 'Being at my peak' tool from our session and used it – it's brilliant.*
- *The 'Being at my peak' tool helps me synchronise with people.*

- *I am more effective in how I use my time and am more prepared for important meetings.*
- *First two sessions were particularly useful. I would not have gotten through that month without the self management tool.*
- *When I do follow the coaching process it works and it fails (I fail???) when I don't.*

This team of sales managers, in a Top 5 Global IT Company, went on to receive an award for being the top performing sales branch across Europe within six months of participating in this endeavour.

*** End of case study ***

Note that, in the case study above, the managers focused on taking themselves (and thus learn how to lead others to do the same) outside their comfort zones. In the subsequent coaching of their people, the managers specifically did not focus on directing their coachees what to do - even though previously, the managers all had successful careers in sales. Instead, the managers coached their direct reports to explore the space beyond their 'boundaries of current success'.

In a nutshell...

- Coaching implies a non-expert and non-directive approach.
- Consulting/mentoring implies an expert and directive approach.

What a Client Seeks: the Overarching Principles
Extract from *Quick Guide: How Top Salespeople Sell*.

• Customers, fundamentally, only ask a salesperson four questions:

1. *Do I trust you?*
2. *What value do you bring to the table?*
3. *Are you the right person/organisation to do business with?*
4. *How does it work (i.e. feature/benefits) or how will we work together?*

Moderate performing salespeople often answer these four questions in reverse order.

Top performers do things better and differently. They:

- Focus first on Questions 1 and 2
- Ask better questions that nurture insight and instil passion
- Guide customers sensitively on a spiral journey in and out of the problems they face. The dualistic nature of this journey inspires action
- Engage the customer to evaluate the consequences of both action and inaction
- Understand and apply what CEOs expect and value from business relationships.

*** End of extract ***

As you work through the sales process for coaching, you will be in a position to contrast it with the overarching principles of *how top salespeople sell* listed above.

You'll then be able to account for how the sales process is so successful.

How to Setup Your First Call

You are calling on someone who is interested in coaching for themselves. You may have been directed by an executive sponsor to meet the client or you may have agreed directly with them to meet for a one to one 'introductory session'.

I set up the first meeting as an *introduction to coaching*, with the express intent of achieving five outcomes for the client:

1. Evaluate outcomes that will make the client's investment (in money, time and energy spent) worthwhile.
2. Gain a clear understanding what value the coaching brings to the client's table.
3. Evaluate me as a suitable coach for them.
4. Provide the client the information they need to decide whether they wish to proceed with the coaching or not. I will ask them at the end of the session how they wish to proceed. I make a point of telling the client that whatever answer they give,

"yes" or "no", is the right answer for them at that point in time.
5. No matter what their decision, the client will walk away with a clearer picture of their priorities over the coming weeks.

I find the above process puts the client at ease and assures them that they will be able to make their own decision without any pressure from me to do so.

Sell Coaching in One Call, via *The Introductory Session*

1. The Interview

I'll share the interview process in two phases. In the first phase, I'll simply list the questions I ask so that you get a feel for the flow of the interview. If you like, you can practice asking the questions on someone willing to help you try them out. The more you practice, the better you become at asking them.

First Phase – Quick Run Through

(I start the list the questions overleaf, on an even numbered page, so that you can photocopy the pages for your own personal use.)

Introductory Session Questions

Tell me about your current role(s), what are your personal responsibilties?

What are the major changes going on in and around your business (or *life,* for personal coaching) *right now and how might these changes impact you? What are the key areas where you personally can or would like to make an impact?*

How will you know if you are being successful? What are some of the measures of success that you either set yourself or are set for you?

If you were to summarise your current situation, what's working well and what would you like to improve or change?

Which aspects of your work do you enjoy most and why?

Which aspects of your work would you say frustrate you most? What tasks do you perform which drain your energy, and why?

What would you say are your strengths?

Over and above what you've already shared, what are some of things you would like to do differently or better, and why?

So if there was one thing that coaching could help you with right now, what would it be? What do you want (instead)? What would be the outcome?

If I were your manager or one of your colleagues- what are some of the things 'I' (i.e. they) would say about you that 'I' value?

If I were your manager or one of your colleagues- what are some of the things 'I' would like you to do more of?

If I were your best friend or partner, what would I say I value about you?

If I were your best friend or partner, what are some of the things 'I' would like you to do more of?

What's important to you outside work?

Thank you - that concludes my questions for now. Is it ok for me to play back what I've heard you say? I'll stop at areas where you can use coaching to help you. Afterwards, you'll be able to get a better feel for how much 'glue' coaching holds for you – ok?

In the second phase, I'll show you a method I use to capture and playback what the client says. I also describe how the 'shape' and sequence of the questions engender trust and value in the eyes of client. Equally important, you, the coach, will learn what to address, 'pleasure and pain points', that will motivate the client to respond positively.

Second Phase – Comments about Each Question

Tell me about your current role(s). What are your personal responsibilities?

This question can be adapted if you want the client to focus on a particular context or project. You start to get a sense for the client's priorities here. The higher the priority, the higher the value of any help you can offer.

What are the major changes going on in and around your business (or *life,* for personal coaching) *right now and how might these changes impact you? What are the key areas where you personally can or would like to make an impact?*

The final question allows you to gently glean the client's priorities. Before that you will be getting information about opportunities and concerns the client has about changes to their environment.

How will you know if you are being successful? Over and above what you've said, what are some of the measures of success that you either set yourself or are set for you?

This technique is called *forward-pacing*. It gets the client to think about success as if it is happening now. *Forward-pacing* bypasses the blocks to success. The 'set yourself' phrase strengthens the client's identity with success and intuitively might start to give them a semblance of how they overcame/bypassed any blocks to get 'here'.

So if you were to summarise your current situation, what's working well and what would you like to improve or change?

This question encourages the client to open up to reveal their most important 'pleasure and pain' points. By obtaining the top three items in each category, the client will be furnishing you with areas they can potentially build on (*what's working well*) and their deepest concerns (*what do you want to improve or change*).

By now, you are solidifying the areas that will elicit a positive response to an offer to help the client.

Which aspects of your work do you enjoy most and why?

Here you'll start to get a feel for the client's preferences to how they think and like to operate. For example, you'll get a feel on whether they are achievement-oriented, people-oriented, task-oriented, strategically-oriented, or a combination of some or all of these facets. Do they like attention to detail or prefer working with the big picture? Do they put achievement before people? Do they look for solid evidence before acting or are they willing to go with their 'gut feel'?

There are no rights and wrongs. You can use the information to frame your subsequent dialogue to match their preferred way of thinking and talking.

Which aspects of your work would you say frustrate you most? What tasks do you perform which drain your energy, and why?

Once again, there are no rights and wrongs. You'll find areas that may disengage the client so don't stay in these for too long. In the fullness of time, these areas, if important, probably need a new and more energised approach. The coaching will help the client to come up with such a new approach. You can cover this in your *playback/review* in the next phase.

Case Study: The Managing Partner Who Hated Repetitive Working

I coached the head of a law firm whose primary ambition was to develop his company to become a leader in European Law and 'Internet Law'. His focus was entirely on restructuring.

The firm's major source of income was processing private health claims, a line of business it had been in for over a hundred years and, even with the introduction of computers and the like, hadn't fundamentally changed much in all that time.

Processing claims was a high volume, low margin and very repetitive transactional business. Yet it was the company's *cash cow*. The people working in the Claims Department were very dissatisfied because the managing partner "seemed to ignore them". The churn of staff in the Claims Department was also on the increase. And yet, it was its contribution to profit that would underpin the funding to the changes the managing partner sought to create.

Upon inspection of his 'least-interest' side, the managing partner used the coaching to create new ways of engaging the members of the Claims Department so that they felt valued and listened to.

*** End of case study ***

What would you say are your strengths?

The answer to this question will give you another perspective of areas the client may wish to build on.

Over and above what you've already said, what are some of things you would like to do differently or better, and why?

This is an opportunity to revisit or discover where the client would like to personally 'up their performance'.

So if there was one thing that coaching could help you with right now, what would it be? What do you want (instead)? What would be the outcome?

At this juncture the client will tell you precisely what the 'number-one-thing' on which they would like your help.

If I were your manager or one of your colleagues- what are some of the things 'I' (i.e. they) *would say about you that 'I' value?*

Having discovered the client's 'map of the world', you now start to explore how they feel they are valued (or not) by the people around them. The answer to this and the next three questions will also give you more information as to how important relationships are to the client.

If I were your manager or one of your colleagues- what are some of the things 'I' would like you to do more of?

It's important to get the client to focus on what others want him to *do more of*. The client may start talking about doing less or stopping something.

Stopping something only creates a void. It doesn't fill the void. For example, being less defensive doesn't imply that someone is going to be more open and honest. Focus on the *more-ofs*.

If I were your best friend or partner, what would I say I value about you?

You now venture questions outside of work to understand the influence that those nearest and dearest to the client have on them.

If I were your best friend or partner, what are some of the things 'I' would like you to do more of?

Here you'll get an insight into any personal areas that the client may feel need addressing.

What's important to you outside work?

It's at this juncture that I share the first insight about the scope of coaching. I talk the client through a sketch as I draw it (see next page).

I talk of how often business people wishing to be more successful do so by working harder and longer hours; at the expense of those nearest and dearest to them in their personal life.

This may be all well and good over a day, even a week – but if the period of work goes on beyond that, it becomes unsustainable. Either the client's wellbeing or the relationship with their nearest and dearest suffers, and in extreme cases one or both break down.

So I tell the client that for coaching to be sustainable it will therefore focus on how they can increase their business contribution and personal well-being simultaneously.

Thank you - that concludes my questions for now. Is it ok for me to play back what I've heard you say? I'll stop at areas which you can use coaching to help you. As a result, you'll be able to get a better feel for how much 'glue' coaching holds for you – is that ok?

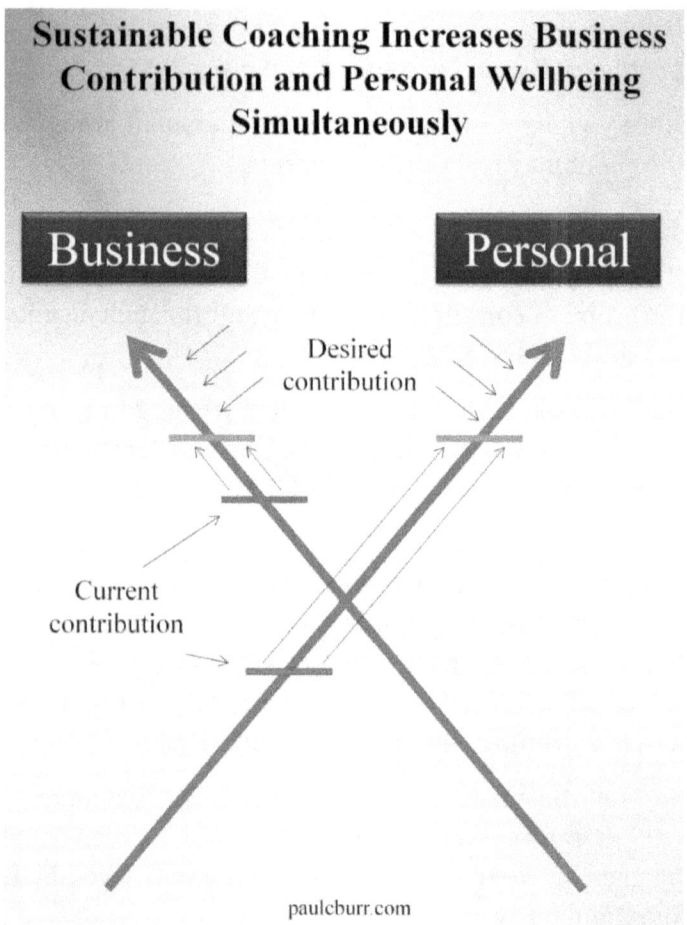

By now the client will already be showing signs that they are eager to hear what you have to say.

Note the interview process normally takes about 45 minutes. I make notes as the client speaks and use the following technique to highlight where the client may want to use coaching.

Very simply, draw a straight line down the right hand side of the page in your note book, to make an inch wide column – an example follows on the next page. Make bullet points of the client's answers to each question to the left of the line.

- If you feel the client talks of something in which they can consider using coaching, mark a single asterisk in the right hand column next to that response.
- If the client speaks of something you feel they will probably want to use coaching to focus on, annotate two asterisks in the right hand column, next to the response.
- If the client speaks of something that you feel strongly they will want to use coaching for, annotate three asterisks in the right column next to the response

The answer to the question, *If there's one thing...*, provides you with at least one 'three-asterisks' answer.

Marking Areas for Potential Focus

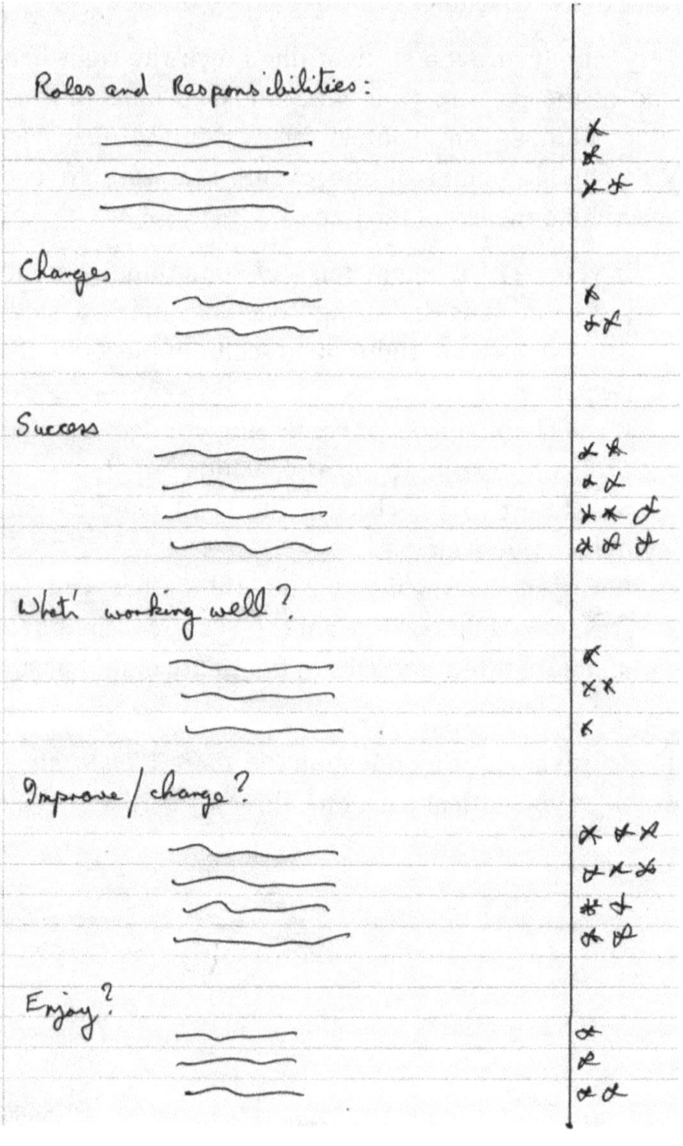
Roles and Responsibilities:
Changes
Success
What's working well?
Improve/change?
Enjoy?

2. Playback/ Review

Proceed by talking the client through your notes. I use phrases like...

You said...

One area that you mentioned a number of times...

You spoke of....

The first thing you answered was........ You can use coaching to improve/give yourself different strategies/come up with new ways to change (insert the situation).

I've worked with a number of clients who wanted to focus on...... (for example: relationships, sales, personal influence, their energy, motivation or enthusiasm).

When you finish, you can summarise the client's priorities and check if there's anything you've missed. Assure the client that *coaching can be used to address all these areas.*

By now, both you and the client should have an understanding of the areas in which coaching can help them.

Case Study: *Let's Skip This, Socrates!*

I once met an impatient CEO, who after twenty minutes or so said... *Look, let's skip this. Sell me coaching!* I handled the CEO's request with a series of implied questions.

I said, *"OK, here's my take. Please interrupt if you feel there's a fault in the logic.*

1. *Your company's business results have been heading south for 'n' years/months?*
2. *What you've done up to now hasn't worked as well as you wanted it to?*
3. *Regardless, you're considering moving on sooner rather than later?*
4. *If you stay, you've implied you have to come up with something different?*
5. *If you move on, you'll be doing something different?*
6. *That's what coaching does, it helps you figure out what to do differently to get different results. Probably things that feel uncomfortable at the moment because if the solution was an intellectual one, you'd have figured it out already. So the question is not whether you want to leave or not. It's 'What am I going to do differently?' Or put another way, 'Do I want to go out with a whimper or a bang?'"*

The CEO bought the coaching programme because I'd used a Socratic series of questions whereby he led himself to the logical conclusion that coaching will help him. (I must admit that it wasn't until I'd analysed what I'd done, using one of my own coaching tools that I discover why I was successful in selling the coaching. Truth be told, I felt 'on the back foot' a bit and was 'shooting from the hip' with a bit of bravado.)

Side-note: Socrates was famous for asking a series of 'yes/no' questions, the answers to which the questionee was inclined to say *"yes"*. With a series of *yes's* the client creates, by affirming, their own logical conclusion to your questioning.

This technique only works if you know the priority issues and opportunities that the client will affirm. If you do not know, then ask permission to ask another three questions (to identify what priority changes need to be made) with the promise that you'll summarise your selling reasons thereafter.

*** End of case study ***

Case study aside, I next say something like... *Have we covered enough ground for me to tell you what coaching is, what coaching is not, and my role as a coach?*

3. Explain What Coaching Is, What It Is Not, and What Needs To Happen To Assure Success

I make the following points about coaching.

It's...

- *One to one*
- *Personal and confidential*

There are no external pass/fail criteria. You give yourself a progress score on how well you are doing at the beginning of every session. Occasionally, I'll be asking you to evaluate the time and commitment you put into the programme so that you can estimate the value you can expect to derive from it.

Coaching is a series of learning experiences aimed at achieving specific outcomes that are important to you. You can think of each coaching session as a primer to help you get the most out of the learning to be had in the period between that session and the next.

Coaching involves exploration and doing things outside what you normally do - so that you can reflect on the different results you get. It's about self discovery, adding to your repertoire and evolving a mindset to deal with the unknown.

Coaching has some time commitments. Each session lasts 2.5 – 3hrs. (I normally propose 7 sessions, each lasting 2.5-3hrs, 10-12 working days apart, for professionals and 10 sessions, each lasting 3-3.5hrs, 15-20 working days apart, for 'executives' with a wide network of people to lead.) *You also spend 1 hour by yourself, within 24 hours of each session to:*

1. Review each coaching tool and schedule the time to conduct any applied learning exercises
2. Step back and see how the tools in that particular session 'knit' together.
3. Step back again and see how all the sessions covered so far 'knit' together. The more connections you make the better you equip yourself to pick the right tools for the right job as and when the coaching is complete. I will be summarising the connections as

we go so you'll always have a good feel for where you are.

To do this reflection, make sure you are in an ideal environment. It would be one free from interruptions, a retreat where you can leave behind psychological baggage from the work you're doing that day, somewhere comfortable and peaceful. Switch off your mobile devices.

My role is non-expert and non-directive. What do I mean by that?

- **Non-expert:** *I don't come along with bags of research and expertise in your business area – and perform some form of gap analysis of how you compare with best practices worldwide. That's more akin to what traditional consulting and mentoring is all about.*

  I am an expert in helping people to step outside the boundaries (to higher success) they set themselves so that they can increase their personal performance by 30%+ in a matter of weeks, sometimes days. That's what I do.

- **Non-directive:** *I do have thirty years experience in corporate business so if I hear you say something that doesn't feel 'good' to me, I may ask your permission to step out of my non-directive coaching role into a directive role. When so, I'll share my experience BUT if I do that I'm deliberately sharing my map of the world not yours. If I attempt to do* *that in my role as a coach, I've found the coaching breaks down. I step out of my coaching role and back into it only with your consent – so that you know when I'm being a coach and when I'm not. OK?*

The coaching is challenging, and provided you choose to work at it, it is very rewarding. Trust yourself, don't pre-judge or over-analyse the reason why you are doing something.

I often deal with analytical people who, as you would perhaps expect, want to know why they are performing an exercise. This is the way traditional training works. You have a clear expectation of an exercise's learning goals at the outset. I don't offer reasons for most of the exercises set, deliberately.

If a goal is set, there is a temptation to stop the exercise once the goal is achieved. That's not how these exercises work. The exercise stops when there's no more learning to be had. I have found that some of these exercises, often the simplest ones, can have a life changing effect on clients when they learn what there is to learn to the 'max'.

Furthermore, there's an analytical pitfall that some people fall into. I give them an exercise and they say something to themselves like, "Oh I can see why Paul's given me this exercise. Therefore I don't need to do it!" We want to avoid that for two reasons:..

1. *The client is already setting subtle boundaries for themselves to the learning.*

2. *The exercises are only of value if they are completed diligently. Having said that, most of the exercises are simple. It's the learning to be had that's subtle and can be profound.*

Some coaching tools will have immediate benefit – others may take time. I've had clients who've come back to me after a year. In one instance a client came back to me after five years to say "thanks". He'd used a specific coaching tool to prepare himself for the interview that would give him his dream job – successfully!

Finally, I work, by and large, with two types of coachees.

1. *The first category put in a 70% commitment. They get 70% of the value from the coaching that they could be getting. They are very satisfied because their business contribution and personal lives have improved measurably. They recommend the coaching to others. And yet, they know that they could have gotten a lot more out of the coaching.*
2. *The second category schedule and complete all the learning exercises diligently; they prioritise this coaching as a tangible opportunity to improve both their business and personal lives. They commit themselves 100% to getting the results they want. They often surpass their outcomes and achieve results they never thought possible in such a short space of time.*

Bottom line, you get out of the coaching what you put into it.

Are there any questions you have at this stage?

So may we proceed to find out what will make the whole programme worthwhile for you?

Thank you.

4. Discover What Will Make Coaching Worthwhile

Apart from the second question (*How will you know if you are successful?*) you have spent most of your time with the client

1. Inside their 'problem space' yet still
2. Outside their 'opportunities-not-yet-taken-nor-fully-defined-space'.

You have indicated how they can use coaching to work on unresolved issues and achieve opportunities open to them. If and when the client is willing to go to this stage; they are ready to tell you what their life will be like with their issues resolved and new opportunities taken. At this point, say...

Imagine it is 3 months from now, right now. You and I are sitting here and you have just completed the coaching programme and all of the learning opportunities diligently. This means it's been the most fantastic programme you could have imagined and has helped you enormously.

I'd like you to write down, on a blank sheet of paper, five to ten outcomes that the coaching has helped you to achieve, as if you have already achieved them. Write them in the present tense, as if they have already happened. That is, start each outcome with the phrase, "I am..." or "I have..."

Use positive phrasing, that is, avoid using the word 'not'. (If the client uses a phrase like 'I no longer feel upset', ask them how they would want to feel instead – accentuate the positive.)

You can think of an outcome as:

1. *A tangible result (e.g. "I have made my sales target")*
2. *An improved relationship (e.g. "I have created an excellent business relationship with X")*
3. *An activity (e.g. "I spend 70% of my time focusing on Y (important matters)...") or...*
4. *A feeling, How you feel (e.g. "I wake up every morning feeling energised and motivated. I feel good about making sales calls, etc.)*

Encourage the client to write three or four outcomes outside of their business life.

Allow the client a few minutes to draft their outcomes. Once complete, ask the client to read them out to you one at a time. Prompt revisions where necessary, ensure all the phrases that the client comes up with are in the present tense and use positive phrasing.

Write down your version of the client's list as it is spoken. Here's an example list of outcomes from an anonymous business client of mine.

Example of Client Outcomes

1. *Each of my team is forecasting £3-5M*
2. *My wedding, honeymoon and holidays are booked.*
3. *I have expanded my social circle with people who have families of children of a similar age to my own.*
4. *I have helped my team to win the top performing team in the UK (if not globally).*
5. *We have broken into new areas in the Public Sector such as xxx and yyy.*
6. *I have influenced X to build and commit herself to a comprehensive business plan for 2014. She is enthusiastic and going for it.*
7. *I have regular reviews with my team. We follow an agreed process.*
8. *I have acquired an experienced B2B salesperson who has hit the deck running.*

*** End of example ***

Once the client has completed the list, with improved phrasing, confirm your understanding of the list by reciting the list, using the above example, as follows.

It is (three months from now). Each member of your team is forecasting £3-5M. Your wedding, honeymoon and holidays are booked. You have expanded your social circle.... and so on.

Make any amendments as instructed by the client. Once the list is complete, ask the client (as follows) to read the list again and...

So as you read down your list of outcomes again, is there anything that you would like to add or change?

Amend the list as guided by the client, re-read it to the client quickly, and reconfirm.

By definition, these outcomes represent the 'n' (in the preceding example, 'n' = 8) *most important things going on in your life right now and over the next three months?*

If the client defers to other important 'things', integrate outcomes for these 'things' in their list - but stick to a list of ten outcomes, maximum.

You now have an agreed list of outcomes, pertaining to the client's most important issues and opportunities, upon which to focus the coaching. Assure the client that in the past you have helped clients (assuming you have) to achieve, if not over-achieve, similar outcomes.

5. Ask the Client if They Wish to Proceed or Not

The client will still be in a 'future state' of mind so now is the time to ask if they wish to proceed or not.

So, may I now ask you, would you like to do this coaching to achieve these outcomes and would you like me to be your coach?

Whatever answer the client gives is right for them and for you.

Calling on an Executive Sponsor

In business, I often called on an executive sponsor who, for instance, might hold the budgetary authority for the coaching programme for which I was being asked to propose. You typically have less time with an Executive Sponsor. The higher you go, the less time they allocate to 'strangers'. So I use a subset of the questions from the *Introductory Session*, reframed for a third person or persons.

Let's say I'm calling on an executive who is interested in coaching for their team or an individual who reports to them. I typically ask a series of questions as follows...

Can you please tell me about your business relationship with X (or the team), i.e. how the responsibilities connect between you?

What are the major changes going on in and around the business right now? How might these changes impact people, your team, or .... (the designated coachee) in particular? How might their perspective of these changes align or differ to yours? What are the key areas where you would like to see them influence these changes or respond to them differently?

How will you know if they are being successful? Over and above tangible business results, how will you see people behaving differently? What behaviours are you expecting or hoping to see?

Coming back to now, if you were to summarise their current situation, what's working well and what would you like to see them improve or change?

If there was one thing that coaching could do for X/these people, what would it be?

I might then follow this up with one or two case studies that provide insights into how coaching has helped clients facing similar issues and opportunities. By insight, I often focus on the inner or emotional journey that people make.

For example, when coaching someone who has been promoted from operations into a more strategic role, one of the issues they might face is to let go of the tasks which they are expert in and renowned for. They are now being asked to fulfil a role that requires focus on strategic change rather than day to day issues.

I inform the sponsor that the success of the programme is down to the commitment of the coachee(s) to 'do the work' and the best way of ascertaining their commitment is via a no-obligation *Introductory Session*, at the end of which the coachee signs up to the coaching and me as their coach – or not.

This takes any responsibility off the sponsor to sell coaching to the people designated for it – and passes the responsibility over to me, which is exactly what I prefer.

I affirm that whatever the answer the coachee arrives at, "yes" or "no", is the right answer for them at that point in time. And indeed, if the answer is "no" then I shall walk away, no charge.

Calling on a CEO

If you're calling on a CEO then they will likely have one question they want answered before you get to ask your questions.

Why am I, personally, talking to you?

For an overview of how to answer this specific question and a summary of what CEOs value and fear, I refer you to the first booklet in this series, *Quick Guide #1 - How Top Salespeople Sell*, Section, *Q2 What value do you bring to the table?*

———

Closing Notes

Whether you are selling to the coachee directly or the executive sponsor, the determining factor, I have found, takes the client into the future and gets them to define success for themselves. In doing this, you take them outside the 'space of current problems' and into the 'space of current opportunities fulfilled'.

Top salespeople, no matter whether they are selling a product or service, ensure that each time the client moves from the present to the future, they are furnished with a fresh insight into how they can be helped. And when they see, hear and feel their problems being solved and opportunities being achieved, with your help better than anyone else; they answer the most vital question they ask of you for themselves, *"Are you the right person for me? Yes!"*

End of main body of article

"Thank you..."

I plan to write further booklets (less-than-sixty-minute-reads) in this series, *Quick Guides to Business*. My next booklet specifies a *B2B Sales, Account Management Template (that's top notch and won't cost you the earth)*.

If you'd like further information about the variety of services I engage in, please visit these websites...

http://paulcburr.com/ ~ extensive and ethereal blog-site that combines business with ancient wisdom

http://www.facebook.com/PaulCBurr ~ over 16,000 followers

http://twitter.com/paulburr

Or mailto: doctapaul@paulcburr.com

Appendix: About me, Paul C Burr

Photo © Stephen Cotterell

I equip people to improve their effectiveness by 30%+ in a matter of weeks, sometimes days.

Business Client: *"I have worked with Paul periodically over the past 8 years to gain solutions to a number of people issues / opportunities. If you are looking for a Personal Coach to make a High Performer / High Performing Team even better (particularly a senior player) – I would not hesitate to recommend him."* - Sandra Ventre, Management Development Director, Reckitt Benckiser (now with Qantas)

Private Client: *"You have been so instrumental in the positive changes in my life, I set quite a few goals, and one by one my goals are being achieved, thanks to you, showing me how."* - Debbie (via Skype) Cape Town, South Africa.

Partial Client List... Accenture, Avery Dennison, Bevan Ashford, Bombardier, BP Marine, Cambridge Technology Partners, Castrol, Charles Burton, European Amateur Natural Bodybuilding Champion, Cisco, Cotoco, CSC, Dept of Trade & Industry (private client), Dixons Group, DTZ, Erevena, Grace Construction, IBM, Microsoft, Newcastle City Council, Northumbria University, Prudential, Reckitt Benckiser, SHL, Staffware (now part of Tibco), United Biscuits, Xerox, Youthforce

The Skills and Passions in Me

Life doesn't get better by chance; it gets better by change.

And change is a journey that's two parts emotional to one part intellectual.

Most of us don't achieve what we set out to achieve at the first attempt. If the outcomes you sought were down to a purely intellectual exercise then you would have achieved them already - would you not? Whether you're a top or moderate performer (or underperforming right now) - every change you make in life is a journey, two parts emotional to one part intellectual. We are twice as likely to hold ourselves back because of self-imposed limiting beliefs we hold about ourselves, our organisation or customers, as opposed to intellectual problems. Put simply, I equip people to tackle challenging emotional journeys; to go beyond the limits to success they impose on themselves and others.

Corporate clients use me as a 'business coach', personal clients probably see me as more of an 'energy healer'. In both cases I help clients to cultivate and apply their innate willpower, imagination, courage and creativity to achieve the business and personal outcomes they seek.

I have over thirty-five years of B2B corporate sales and management experience, sixteen years of which overlap with my business and personal coaching work. I have a PhD in Statistics and a First Class Honours Degree in Mathematics. I'm qualified as a Master Practitioner in NLP, this/past life regression and hypnotherapy.

I give talks (and appear on talk shows) on selling, executive coaching, Neuro-Linguistic Programming (NLP), ancient wisdom, football and more ethereal subjects – sometimes to the same audience!

I write books, blogs and am now partway through a series of business articles based upon my own original research, experience and observations in corporate and small/medium sized businesses.

I study and practice ancient wisdom, astrology, casting runes, dowsing, the I Ching and the Tarot.

I love listening to music – rock, jazz, country... you name it. I sing a bit too.

I'm a passionate football fan of Newcastle United Football Club, in "Geordieland", in The North-East of England.

My Promise:

The material I use is powerful, very powerful. I know of nothing quicker or more effective. It's non-mainstream - which means you get non-mainstream results.

The Author in Me...
Quick Guides to Business, Volumes I - V

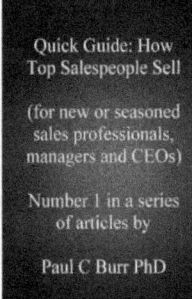
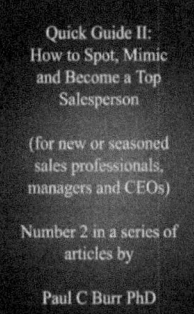
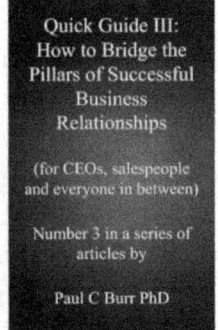
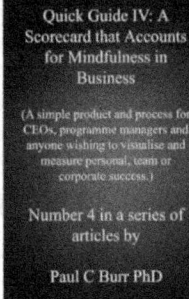
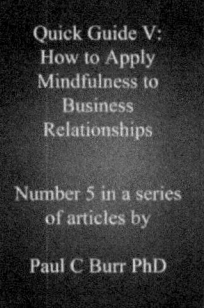

Quick Guide – How Top Salespeople Sell

- *"...a must read for both novice salespeople and the experienced...."* - Author, Chiahou Zhang
- *"I loved it... it was great. I've encouraged many of my directors to buy a copy as it's very pertinent to my company"* - paraphrased from a top

performing B2B salesperson for a global IT Services organisation

- *"I work for a large American IT company, and can say this is a hugely powerful book to articulate what is required to get to Board level. To really understand what the CEO and C level executive summarise as valuable and impactful, and in a condensed easy-to-digest format, is phenomenal. I find Paul C Burr's style of writing easier to digest and apply in any sales situation; it crystallises where the true business value add is delivered and how you really have strategic partnerships. I have just got number 2 book and look forward to reading this with excitement - which is saying something as my concentration span can be limited. Thank you."* - Amy Lambkin, 5-stars, book review

Quick Guide II - How to Spot, Mimic and Become a Top Salesperson

Quick Guide III - How to Bridge the Pillars of Successful Business Relationships

Quick Guide IV – A Scorecard that Accounts for Mindfulness in Business

Quick Guide V – How to Apply Mindfulness to Business Relationships

Learn to Love and Be Loved in Return

"Uplifting: this is one of those books that arrives in your life at just the right time, when you need it most. The author is able to convey a very deep and meaningful message in an easy to read and understand format with a step by step guide on how to achieve this. The best type of love is unconditional and what better place to start than with yourself." - Rhedd, 5-stars, book review

2012: a twist in the tail, a novel with spiritual insights

"This is a compelling story for our troubled times. Paul C Burr writes with passion and compassion about moral uncertainties and the quest for salvation and spiritual fulfilment. Go with the flow, trust your inner-self and enjoy this humane and optimistic tale." - Professor John Ditch, York, UK.

"This is a gripping read - beautiful, insightful and very enjoyable. I found phrases and thoughts staying with me, and becoming part of my understanding of the world." - Caroline Eveleigh, *Getting to Excellent*

Defrag your Soul

"You should be proud of DYS Paul. I think it is amazing and I'm still thinking hard about what you've written." - Amanda Giles, Author

"DYS whispered to me, 'take heart, be aware, let your journey this far nourish your inner self to be at peace, to love and to shine as your journey continues'." - Penelope Walsh, Book Review

The Mystique to the Game of Life (and Unrequited Love)

"Revelatory - the Mystique to the Game of Life drew me in. I wanted to carry on reading as much as I wanted to stop and do the exercises! It struck a number of chords with me, and just through reading the book I became aware of some very important things - habits, conditioning, behaviours - that I needed to address to make my life and my relationships happier and healthier. The author has a way of writing that reaches deep down into your heart; it gets you in that feeling place. His writing is more than words on a page. It's more a guide that leads us to recognise, deal with and move on from whatever may be holding us back." - Amazon 5 star review.

For The Love of Lilith & How to Put Love into Practice (and Non-attach Yourself to It)

"For the Love of Lilith is a powerful tool to enhance the awareness, appreciation and enjoyment of living and loving in harmony. It is a book that can be used to strengthen and reinforce areas of my life and make sense of the non-sense that can accompany me in matters of the heart." - Amazon 5 star review.

www.ingramcontent.com/pod-product-compliance
Lightning Source LLC
Chambersburg PA
CBHW071817170526
45167CB00003B/1347